Easy Victims to the Charitable Deceptions of Nostalgia

Easy Victims to the Charitable Deceptions of Nostalgia

— *poems* —

Emily Schulten

WHITE PINE PRESS / BUFFALO, NEW YORK

White Pine Press
P.O. Box 236
Buffalo, NY 14201
www.whitepine.org

Publication of this book was supported by public funds from
the New York State Council on the Arts, with the support
of Governor Kathy Hochul and the New York State Legislature,
a State Agency.

Acknowledgements: See page 84.

Cover Image: "Boat stranded near Key West, Florida." tmckinley,
Shutterstock.

Printed and bound in the United States of America.

ISBN 978-1-945680-76-2

Library of Congress Control Number: 2024930191

for Dakin

CONTENTS

As for me, I knew then that for the rest of my life I would never stop missing the thunder at three in the afternoon.

–Gabriel Garcia Marquez,
Living to Tell the Tale

Ode to Fetal Sharks in Jars

Dakin misses the days when they sold the preserved
fetal sharks up and down the main drag. As a kid

he gazed for long stretches of time at dozens
of upturned faces in blue liquid – not in water,

not even close to being something of the body,
not even close to being something of the sea –
noses to the sky, without air, frowning.

Their wide eyes and undeveloped arms in permanent
and suspended surprise, grotesque and plastic.

Their solitude was his, too, when fewer people
peopled his streets, when space and silence
existed and these tchotchkes dotted the state
straight up the panhandle in a line of citrus stand signs:

towering oranges eclipsing the sun and pineapples
made of metal and neon, their leaves great enough for osprey
to make nests in, and be left alone, mostly.

A map for sleepy summer drives
        in unbearable heat, straight down
                to the place of his birth, a map he can't travel now –

a quiet as hard to put a finger on as nostalgia.

Now, everywhere, there is noise.
Not the sound of sea. Not the sound of breeze.

Now, everywhere, there is the sound of bodies never suspended
for long and buildings always building upward to get us all –
everyone who can possibly fit – closer to the sunset, the divine

and commercial sunset, more brilliantly red and pink
by the summer (and it's always summer) day.

There used to be siestas.
And he remembers them.

In the afternoon, in August, his eyes
surveyed the displays of sharks
that would always be young and never be
swimming. The streets were emptied

and the storefronts cleared,
the men home in hammocks, their chests undressed
and bellies bared to the shade of the mango trees
and their leaves, and they shook,
                    and you could hear them.

El Lector

Key West

Your father tells lies about how it began,
your father tells it that he was *El Lector*.

He walked the aisles of immigrants,
their hands browned and fists sore,
to stand above them on *la tribuna*, in the smoke, revered.
He read Cervantes emphatic with gesture,
his Castilian brought life to *La Voz de la Suciedad*.

You're as certain this isn't the truth
as your father's certain it is. In your version,
your great-grandfather comes from Cuba
and he is merely one of those cigar rollers.

But narrative is all that's left, so much
of where you were born only exists in folktale.

The pattern of barreling down to build more
and higher has made a mass-produced tropic
of your birthplace and exiled to memory
all that is native, your legacy an oral lore,
a telephone-game mythology.

The only truth you know is that you are confined
to this island, set in the coral stone of your birth.

The past only foretells when read backward.

So I listen to you tell me your story in circles,
a curse our children will inherit:
their chronicle a catacomb that can't be unearthed.

Handling the Wind

Before your mother was a mother, she took a job sewing sails
in a loft on Greene, near the harbor. This is how
her hands touched the wind.
                                        In the quiet of dust,

she needled with small strokes the canvas
that would carry men across oceans.

Before knowing she would stay,
before her husband and her son,
                        she hemmed and patched
each broad piece with an affection for adventure
that permeated the fabric
that would manipulate the air,

pushing ships away from the Gulf,
maybe to come back, maybe not.

Perhaps she gave those ships
all of her wandering
there was to give.
Years later, she recalls,
with joy seldom replicated,
the work that's all but obsolete now.

Sail lofts have all closed, the work is done
by factories a hundred miles from the island –

there are fewer hands to guide the wind,
there is a greater divide between man and sky,
and there are so many ways to be trapped on an island.

The Ballad of the Ground

It all changed when the ground became rubble
beneath their feet, the explosion cracking open

the earth and the road splayed wide, jackknifed
before them, flying in bits of pebble overhead

that would land, eventually, on the water:
the facsimile terrain to make the small island

into new island, more island. This is where Max —
somehow still a boy, despite the years —

lives now, in repurposed Naval housing, concrete
painted pink and mint, made into sanitariums.

The island is more real here somehow,
but without history — this doubling

making two towns, one for native sons,
where people search for and cling to

what's past. And one for people who need
a place to keep a suitcase for a week. Downtown

where everything is old, the roads meet
two oceans with ease, a stretch of pavement

uncracked, but beneath it, hollow and exploded,
are the remnants of legacy. His family

passed down their homes from generation
to generation — you point them out

when we walk by. Now, they are empty
or used for transient rentals,

the once-white siding newsprint
telling a smudged story of his family

leaving the island — dying or fleeing.
He's the only one left. He calls you

sometimes, tells you stories about who he is
now. You've been told not to believe him.

Once he asked for a ride to see the field
where as boys you'd ride bikes, kick at dirt

and throw baseballs. You showed him
the houses built there and explained

that the field doesn't exist. He didn't believe.
He wandered the sidewalk corridors until dark,

and then got back into your car, smiling, quiet.
He refuses to lose his history, carries a shard

of his grandmother's china in his pocket, buries
his great-grandfather's sunken-ship gold to grow

the past back, to show you it still exists. He is the soil
of the island, his head so full of fragments of coral,

the rubble so thinned he can't find his footing,
can't tell the earth he came from without tasting it.

To Make Paradise Out of Paradise

I

Your twisted, breathing, overlapping roots
and white sand swatches in thistle and spray
came after coral forest, bright and bathed,
came after glacial melting, when sea moved.
You came from decay, from the skeletons
of reef, anemone, and crustacean.
Ocean drops, currents follow your boundary.
Ocean drops, the wind finds your new body.
Your life becomes the heron and ibis
scratching at your rock and climbing your skies.
In your low places, the lagoons and ponds
remain, amble through your scrub and stray frond
toward your knife-sharp shore. Everything that grew
after, your wind's last breath of solitude.

II

After your wind's last breath of solitude,
your story is ghosts. It's told from the mounds,
ceremony sites, burials, bones, food
remains, masks, conch shells, trash left underground
by the Calusas who were left slaughtered
on your shore, whitewashed coral of their bones
becoming your landscape. They ate sea grapes,
dug canoes from hollowed-out cypress, and
waded flats with palm-web nets to catch your
conch, your turtles, your lobster. They wove clothes
from your grass and worshiped from three souls formed
in the eye, reflection, and shadow. They
lived this way until stronger tribes came and
clouds of arrows left only bodies, breeze.

III

Clouds of arrows left only bodies, breeze,
and from a distance Ponce de Leon passed,
navigating the tangle of prop roots
and twisted, dark canopy of mangrove,
the sharp bed beneath. The rocks that rose from
your green water reminded him of the
bodies of his suffering men, he christened you
Los Martíres, like the conqueror lives lost.
Many pilfered your water then. Pirates
came for sunk ships, Bahamians for wood,
Cubans for fish — dried, salted goliaths.
They hefted their bounty back home, turning
their backs toward Norte de Havana, making
the last sound of twilight their pushing waves.

IV

The last sound of twilight, their pushing waves,
'til new men came, arguing, to lay claim.
Even then, more thought you belonged to them
than there was for you to give. In attempt
to make you theirs, they drew a map, its shape
like a fish, surrounded. They found emeralds
and mounds of shells and took them away, found
those bones, corrupted your name so they could
understand, *Cayo Hueso* to *Key West*.
You were carved into fourths, sold to men who
saw what could be sold in your deep harbor,
groped your ponds, lagoons, low and high hammocks.
They came next with the pole and flag, people
hushed beneath its far-cast, blinking shadow.

V

Hushed beneath its far-cast, blinking shadow,
and now divided, men built planked bridges
from one shore to another, over ponds.
They cut your trees and cacti, took away
your vines and burned your brush, cleared all traces
of your wilds. You were a city. Ship captains made
houses where woods had been, they filled salt ponds
and lagoons with sand, and from your downed trees
they built boats, and your water made them rich.
They stole from the ships run aground by your
chains of reef and shoals, ships ripped end to end,
sinking in unlit, unforgiving sea.
From the south, more came ready to claim
the wrecks, splayed wide, glistening in your flats.

VI

The wrecks, splayed wide and glistening in your flats,
supplied settlers with treasures from ships' holds:
bronze, cut-glass chandeliers, mirrored armoires,
claw-foot Empire sofas. The town made law
and business of wrecks. The Navy made port
to take taxes. Hook boats pushed through shallows
stabbing sponges to bring from the mangroves
to harbor by sunset. Near there were heaped
hordes of sea turtles, dead or dying. By
day's end, what had been underwater was
piled onto the docks, high enough to meet
the horizon at sunset, ready to
be checked and counted, shipped and sold. The town's
men gazed toward sinking sun, still more gazed in.

VII

Men gazed toward sinking sun. Still more gazed in
from the south, seeking separation from
Spain. Émigrés saw the tip of the pier,
their refugee shapes grew taller until
their faces became familiar and their
shoulders close enough for embrace, far from
Guerra Grande. Exiles spilled into your
streets: parades, processions. Ruffled rumba
shirts and dresses, drumbeat, bolero, sounds
so loud they cracked open the very island,
leading the parade into its belly of coral,
into a time before the land lifted its head
above water, La Banda Libertad's
songs vibrating those first-discovered bones.

VIII

Songs vibrating those first-discovered bones
could be heard in the corner groceries,
inside the bakeries, heading toward the wood-
limbed buildings with windows wide, peeking in
at men seated in rows and rolling, their
price paid per cigar. Your channels opened
to embrace more, Bahamians came to
settle, now, drawn by your waters' blooming
sponges, swollen pink and orange, after
their own pineapple ground had worn too thin
to provide. They hammered planks into boats
and sewed sails, found new freedoms. Their roots here
are strong, but banyan, ground too hard to dig, so
histories wrap and choke toward their own leaves.

IX

Histories wrap and choke toward their own leaves
in cigar plants now bare of all but hush
and sun burns water in ports where once great
ships made shadows. One hundred years rising
only to fall, the sound of the train, only then
becoming familiar, now echo. Men
stopped carrying away trash. It heaped in
the streets by cottages whose shingles hung
askew and steps were cracked, crumbled concrete.
Music stopped. Air hushed. Defeated, your
people pled that the state take over town,
its people moved and city left for wind.
Instead, a deal — a town saved by a plan
to make paradise out of paradise.

X

To make paradise out of paradise,
first, they brought in artists, set up easels
to turn panoramas to brochures.
They taught locals to make jewelry to sell
from shells, your coral and palm stage perfect
backdrop to present the show – look at the
boys carrying fish from harbor, the man
blowing songs from a conch, hear the laúd
in the night clubs the New Deal built. See how
they make this island two: little houses
or huge hotels, men who throw coins into
the sea to watch local boys run after.
This is how a place becomes a postcard,
the end of the road, end of a rainbow.

XI

The end of the road, end of a rainbow
where now pavement's laid, anyone can get
here. Many are the lost who decide to
go until there's no more road, so they stare
outward, wanting more than anything for
there to be some new magic emerging
from the water. Their presence is a search,
and the water, murkier after dark,
hallucinates in reflection, making
for tides of streetwalkers, sailors, dancers
and shrimpers, loners nightlong, distorting
this place to what they'd dreamed it'd be. It's
a dream, waking in sweats, discovering
their last chance to seek what doesn't exist.

XII

Their last chance to seek what doesn't exist
makes of palm canopies tents for looting
the night. Writers and painters create
the perfect scene, perfect for prowling their lives.
Soon, this was everybody's paradise:
if you can dream it, it will be. Look, step
past the man sooted in salt, see the sea?
Sip and watch the sunset there. It's all yours,
it's for sale. The exiles, artists, you
can count on their ghosts, make believe
is buried beneath those condo-gods rising
to face the sun. Tours will tell stories,
a folklore of half-truths, cleaned-up tale of
white picket fences, sand and conch façade.

XIII

White picket fences, sand and conch façade,
tropical gardens where local landscapers
spend more time than the name on the deed. Peek
past tall gates, between planks to see slivers and
slants of mansions not fathomable to the
rows of shotgun conch cottages still standing,
to the people both born and exiled here,
no longer able to find the city they were born to.
The heavy reef sinks slowly where once there was
water, now concrete, over which the landscapers,
bartenders and tour guides ride a bus
home, an island or two away from the
buzzed and swaying tourists, as the shrinking
last lights of Duval grow dim at first sun.

XIV

Last lights of Duval grow dim at first sun,
the island's only quiet space of day.
The curtain down, street sweepers clear away
the debris of yesterday. And you turn
like this too, a continuing toil
to carry the water back over all
of this again. Your wind has been enough
to strip people bare, your surge enough
to swallow houses whole. Your tide rises
in splashes of storm on cement sea walls
to claim what will be yours again – slowly,
your wet fingertips crawling further up
the spine of your coral island to meet
your twisted, breathing, overlapping roots.

XV

The twisted, breathing, overlapping roots,
and your wind's last breath of solitude, brought
clouds of arrows leaving only bodies, breeze,
the last sound of twilight, the pushing waves.
Hushed beneath a far-cast, blinking shadow,
the wrecks, splayed wide, glistened in your flats and
men gazed out at sinking suns, while still more gazed in.
Songs vibrated those first-discovered bones, whose
histories wrap and choke toward their own leaves
to make paradise out of paradise
at the end of the road, end of a rainbow,
the last chance to seek what doesn't exist: those
white picket fences and sand and conch façades
as the lights of Duval are growing dim at first sun.

We'll All Be Drowned

All at once something like scales fell from Saul's eyes, and he could see again.
—*The Holy Bible: International Standard Version*

Lean your ear close to the tide, my dear, learn the sound
of swallowing. The scales bind men's eyes now,
afraid to see, that one day soon we'll all be drowned.

The algae line on the brick rises toward the cannon's mouth,
a quiet advance moves unnoticed to take three forts.
Lean your ear close to the tide, my dear, learn the sound

of the language your children will know, the muted
depth where you will kneel when it's thigh deep, too
afraid to see that one day soon we'll all be drowned.

Gather where that steeple raises a star to the sky, but don't
pray, picture on its angles where the sea grass will snag,
and lean your ear close to the tide, my dear, learn the sound,

prepare now for the fools who thought they'd built heaven
to paddle among the fish in the streets, their own floundering,
afraid to see that one day soon we'd all be drowned.

Watch wood floors buckle, stone gardens grow, submit
to the glass breaking, everything turning blue, and
lean your ear close to the tide, my dear, learn the sound
and see, that one day soon we'll all be drowned.

Changing as quickly as you blink

Lovebirds

Angharad tells me about her lovebird who's killed his partners
       three times
in the night, a species named for its need of one other. But this bird,

though made for monogamy, can't help but thrust his sharp, long
beak into each mate — once it was the chest, two times the neck.

Perhaps it's the crap beneath the perch, piling up. Maybe she never
sweeps up her bright green, molted feathers, or he wonders what one

with an orange chest might have to offer. It's his duty, too, to feed her,
to chew and regurgitate, chew and regurgitate. To have someone

depend on you so wildly and in such vivid color, with such songful
       praise!
But probably, he's just scared he may need her song too much, her caw

along with his. That he's made for this frightens him. New love,
do not be surprised if our bed sprouts copper bars, arching over
       our heads

in the dark, a temple to expectation, its only door embellished with
       metal doves,
our only cover synthetic ivy. Too pretty not to be a trap, but we are
       fooled.

In the morning one of us may be gone, the stabbing ache of need
       too biting
not to bite back, our last song the echo of pierced cry, in harmony.

The Dangers of Touching

The guide warns us against the dangers of touching
the cave's stalactites growing in underground dark,
longer with the seeping water, almost as if it would be soft
if you touch it, blooming cotton ready to fall in.

The cave's stalactites growing in underground dark
take us home, to where the reef's delicate coral dies
if you touch it, blooming cotton ready to fall in,
inside itself, the oils of your palm poison to the sea-forest.

Take us home, to where the reef's delicate coral dies
and we're powerless and we're tempted to push the earth
inside itself, the oils of your palm poison to the sea-forest
and to cave teeth. We go into our room instead,

and we're powerless and we're tempted to push the earth
with our bodies, our palms pressed to our skin, the sea-forest
and the cave teeth come into our room instead,
where we ignore the warning against the dangers of touching.

Murmuration

If we move with the fluidity of starlings,
like a puddle of clippings in the air that shape-
shifts but never falls hard to the ground,

if we sense enough of each other to know
in which direction to fly away from being
preyed upon, but never from one another,

in swirls and with the unshakable faith
that wherever we turn we will be synchronal,
miming in a language only our bodies

comprehend the intention of our design,
the spaces we will fill up and disappear from.
We will be spirals and domes, we will make

mountains and geysers and open mouths
in the sky, an unnoticed eclipse at twilight
as our bodies thrum and flutter without

leading, only the sense of same direction,
of how moving together this way
makes us impenetrable to hawk and falcon,

how having no intention of place or time
allows us to tighten our formation, but leave
space enough not to tangle feather or wing.

Our Life a Stereoscope

Because of you, I am dying. Like the rat
our landlord is poisoning to make us feel
more comfortable where we sleep at night,
my days are numbered. I know it more

each night I try to sleep on your rising,
falling chest. When you search my eyes
I see reflected in them two long, shining
caskets. These tiny pictures have grown

clearer the longer I've let myself look,
our life a stereoscope, the other slides
changing as quickly as you blink, the back-
drops shifting to sun-heat, to yellow leaves

before I can focus clearly, before I can
make out the shapes of our bodies clinging
more tightly to one another, until there is
nothing to hold, nothing to touch, nothing

to see but the long box on the frozen ground.
You're explaining how the bait works inside
the small body of our house rat, how he'll bleed,
and I stop you. I already know.

Love Poem, Interment

A mud-chunk-covered iguana crawls out of one
of the stone beds mounted on top of the coral.
Your family history an ode in boxes: the cramped
galley for coming from Cuba, the stamped and hinged
for an hour's rolled cigars, and these at our feet now,
for sleep. One tomb is smaller, tilting out
of the ground, as if it is giving her back to us.

Miles away my father is feeding the magnolia
that hovers above his grave in the soft dirt
where his body is deep now, his dry skin
and cartilage fertilizer for the leather and lemon.
Their white swells for only a few days, then brown,
dropping its fruit pit hard, scattering red seeds.

Nearby, past the wrought iron Stars of David,
a loud backhoe grabs the ground to make a place
among the *Brothers of Zion*. There are so many
interpretations of family. What is excavated now
will become a tower, stacked stories, intersecting lives.

I say to burn and you say to bury, and the rest
we agree on — we will become nothing together,
we will expose the entirety of our bones,
to dry and be bleached white in the sun.

Multilingual

My dear one talks in his sleep, a clearer Spanish
than he can manage when he's awake. I can't

understand the words much less the sentences,
and more than once I've asked him if these strung

together phrases are love for another woman –
someone before me, with sharp features and

the unattainable loveliness I lost to him long ago.
Someone who could understand, even taught him,

one or two of these middle-of-the-night words.
I've tried before to look them up, for a while kept

a pocket translation guide at the bedside, under
some notes and hoping not to be discovered.

But even he doesn't know how it could be
that he manages the words without a stutter,

without fumbling for conjugation. He tells me
it used to be screams, a fear rooted so deep

within him that it must come from a past life,
filling the whole house with unholy noise.

The words, then, must come from another
lifetime, too, I tell him, and I ask him to please

speak of me in his next life, in any tongue
he can manage, in the middle of the night

and next to any woman he might find in his bed.
He promises to torment them all with translations

of our life, the way he torments my nights
with mysteries he's made secrets of by morning.

I Dreamt You Gave Me a Thesaurus

I dreamt you gave me a thesaurus –
unabridged and full
of every word I would ever need
to say *thank you*, to say
I owe you the way I owe you
the way I see my life, *duration,*
existence, one's born days.

It was navy and leather bound
with snaked-skin that I could feel
even in my dream-hands,
and it had moons in the pages
where I could put my finger and open
to the letter that I touched
to lead to words that have touched me
like yesterday
lead to you
lead to tomorrow
lead to this heavy volume.
See: *Capacity*. See: *Loudness*. See:
Bulk. See: *Contents*, but see
the words move on the page
so that *content* never stays the same,
the way the book of words evaporated
when I woke up and you were there
not quite on your pillow anymore
but between our cushions.
Look, now it says *fulfilled.*

Big Pine Key State Prison

The day before our wedding,
we decided to break into the prison
after reading a headline that it had been

shuttered, the men emptied from cells,
the halls filled by the kind of quiet and echo
you could almost touch.

You pried where a board looked loose,
your knuckles scraped and bled
where you pushed inside.
Getting in was the hardest part.

There were no heavy bars
in the hallways,
only doors, left open forever,
the inside becoming freer
than the outside had been.

We whispered — afraid
even the emptiness would hear us —
about how boundaries work
both ways, letting someone in so easily
confused with locking someone inside.
We shouted to hear who was louder,
how our voices blended in the air
then were gone.

The floors weren't concrete
and stained with the memory of bodies,
as I expected, but artifacts made nests
in the corners of each room,
what had been taped in front of beds
and hidden inside books
we rummaged through.

I found a sketch of a snow-scape
and some glossy prints
torn from the wall: a family
in the sunshine. I imagined them
on a farm, wide open space.
We couldn't tell by looking
which one was the prisoner
but we each guessed, deciding finally
he may not be in there at all.

When My Stepbrother Went Missing

I found out in a news clip, sent from someone
I didn't know well: A whole person lost, a shadow,

dissipated into cloud (like my friend who pictures
the tumor in her sister's leg, shrinking, and it works),
the heat of blood there, then gone.

There were lights, plane blades,
large groups breaking
into small groups, into grids.
They were dragging the creek, shining
white lights onto ground, onto tree limbs,
onto hollowed out nighttime.

But he was nowhere. Six feet
and two inches of man,
now wind.

What would you do,
you ask, *if you woke up,*
and I was missing?

I want to tell you I would find you,
even if it meant my whole life was a search.
Even if what I found was only remains.

I would dream you, dream you out of coral
until the sand gave slack enough
to become your body. I would build you
out of stilt roots and wire. No,
out of bark and clay. No,
out of even less, from a storm's first gust.

But it's a lie. We both know
I would come to waking each morning without wailing,
soon without crying at all, and then just without,
smoothing the bedcovers, petting the panting dog.

It took two days to find my stepbrother.
He crawled out of the mouth of a cave
where he'd slept, climbed the shale rock
and knocked softly on a farmhouse door,
oblivious to what had happened in the night.

400 Portraits

They were together for 20 years until his death, during
which time he created over 400 portraits of her.
—WYNC News

See how many different ways Jacqueline looked to him
and at him. Each time he saw something new and worthy
of the canvas, the brush. This is the only woman we see
Pablo transform for. Day after day he tried to capture her, new.

She is both bright and ashen, charcoal and smear, as she ages
twenty years on twenty times as many easels. He saw her in shades
of brown, her eyes gazing in all directions. (Looking for whom?)
He saw her adorned by crowns of flowers, rooms of flowers.

He placed a rose in her hand every day for 182 days, a lattice of roses
before her the first time he composed her, when she was his new wife.
He saw her bared down, unadorned, naked. He painted her in pieces,
in parts, in catlike angles and edges. In shadow. In light.

Or was he trying to see her, his longest search? Watching him die,
she said of him, *I saw a pink face become grey.* His last living art.
When he was completely covered with dirt and snow, she spread
the entirety of her ache across the length of his grave, and slept this
          way –
another layer of body, another layer of sleet. Everything was cold.

Who is found there, then, in those 400 portraits of Jacqueline –
is it him or her that each stroke, scratch, fleck of dust divulges? The
          fury
of obsession to render your own love, already so perfect in its flawed
and many faces, exposes at last what one cannot make sense of:

your face the cave painting and indecipherable message repeated
on every ever-changing inch of the pink and grey inside of my body.

Ghosts are in these afternoon songs of torment

Sunday Morning

Everything is lilac and acrid,
men hover around the woman
in the window making con leches
and cheese toast. They talk
of weather and the plans
for dredging or for housing —
everyone who is here is also looking
for a way to be here. I am looking
at the diamond pattern on my sheets,
the young girl smacking the glass
where my clothes circle and press
against the front of the machine,
and I am grunting loudly
in the direction of the man beneath
the tracking of the industrial door
as he lights a cigarette and my load
dings and counts down from 30.
Every time, hefting the wet clothes
to the dryer is like moving that week
of my life into whatever space is not
being used — dropping grey lace
panties onto the floor where
the owner pretends not to notice them,
settling for the kind of clean that
carries the hint of Winstons
and grease. One of the plastic baskets
breaks and pinches my hand,
so full of what needs freshening.
At home, I'll dress the bed and cover
my body and carry with me the smoker
and the men and the coffee
and the woman in the window

and the unattended child
into the next week, untethered
to anything except for what's
already been, what will be embedded
despite trying to wash it away.

Summer Storms

We can hear the cries of heat rage
coming from that cottage next door
'round midafternoon. It's the lady
the other neighbors say is crazy,

but we know — she is alone
and she is fevered
like the rest of us. It's the fever
that strands people here,

marking notches in the window frame
for each one that's gone north,
running a finger over the tracks
of the people who may never come back.

Their ghosts are in these afternoon
songs of torment. As for us,
we lock the doors in summer —
not to keep others out

but to keep ourselves in. We take off
more clothes by the hour, scream
at each other, put our ears to the door
to listen for the fits that might come

from outside. (Once, a gunshot, it became
the night-gossip in bars.) We empty
bottles of beer until our bellies distend,
and we lie down, flat on the floor,

our bodies perfectly straight and not
touching, waiting for the dark
to roll in long enough to bring the night
jasmine and exorcise the furies.

The Motorcycle Accident
Key West, 1984

When you were a boy, the man would tell you
to pick out the colored marbles among the pebbles
in his driveway down the lane, occupying you for hours
while your mother drank wine with the man on his porch.

Busy with what was marble
and what was merely stone,
you were too distracted to see
the man's slow decline.

When the man died,
the grief was hard like a stone in the hand of a child
who's discovering for the first time what *hard* means -

Your parents *said* the man had driven a motorcycle
too fast and too leaning, and when it drew a crescent-
shaped line in the gravel, the man was thrown.

Now, you knew what it felt like
to watch your parents cry,
and you thought you should cry too,
in the dark of your room, rubbernecking your gaze
though the window to see the man's absence
on his porch. But you couldn't see.

Afterward, when you'd knock around
the neighborhood, before you became a man,
you never found marbles anymore, only sand.

Ice Diving

Louisville, 1968

At seventeen, he didn't have permission
like his friends to go under the ice,
to dive down and see
what the river held secret in winter.

So he sat on the bank instead, bundled
and waiting for the two divers
to come up from the jagged manhole
they'd made, their bodies
blue as the water under snow.

My father could not have made sense
of their swimming, the light coming in slits between
clouds made by clumps of snow above them,
could not have seen the world that opened
up to them, the daisies growing in January
on the river's floor,
the sunken tires in the lifeless quiet
reflecting off the ice-ceiling above them.

My father only saw around him
the brown of winter, the clouds that build
in waves on waves of grey,
branches bearing nothing but yearning
for spring, for the frost to melt away
the suffocation coating their limbs.

When they descended, looking up
at my father, smiling and still such boys,
untethered and unaware
                    that the air wouldn't last

as long, and the opening would become
impossible to find, the way my father's friends
became impossible to find,
and he waited.

Eventually worrying,
eventually walking the perimeter,
he shouted for echo's sake
their names. But their heads never emerged
from their hole. In the icy blue of winter,

their mouths froze open to scream his name –
an image fossilized in my father's memory,
as permanent in his brain as the limestone bed
where his friends went to final sleep.

The Poem I Can't Write

Because while we're trying to get pregnant,
we do not, and so the painting in the museum

did not prophesy conception. In it, two
whale sharks swim, mouths open in a mantle

of squid, catching as many as they can, ·
and the water meets the night sky, full moon

illuminating the earth straight through
to the ocean floor. When we passed it,

I felt such certainty. Months before,
you'd looked at me in a sweaty bar downtown

and reminded me we'd be lousy parents,
I was out of work and renting rooms

from whatever friend would let me, and you
didn't own any furniture, you slept on an air

mattress and kept your most important books
and notes in piles in the corners of your studio.

But it doesn't work when I try this way
to convince myself that it's for the best,

I still feel the empty crescent where inside me
should be full, I read the world for its clues,

the painting calling to me like a tarot card,
like the Empress. I planned to remember

the painting, and write in all the vivid colors
in my head about how those submerged

wide-mouths predicted a baby that day,
and while I waited I too was under water,

without breath, learning to let go of gravity,
of stories I won't tell.

Capilla

It's important their small faces face the street, lit up
at night, their solemn eyes to the sky, blinded

by the street lamp, illuminated by yellow plastic lilies.
We are trying faith in beads, in dance, in the *promesa*,

for fertility. You lug three pieces of heavy fir onto
your shoulder, I follow you with a candle, clutching

a worn and fragile swath of cloth that, sworn to be a relic,
your grandmother handed to you when you saw her last.

At home, you teach yourself the rhythm of a saw —
its motion not unlike our penance, pressing forward

with all your strength toward the wood, pulling back
in repetition, progress nearly unnoticeable, the sweat

dripping from your forehead — no, from your entire torso.
I choose a pale blue for the paint, the one I remember

from the church as a child, from draped fabric veils
made of stone. We are hoping for an opening,

a crack in the sky to provide for the blessing
our bodies have hoped for each month.

But each month my body, a disappointment.
Our statue of Saint Francis arrives as you are finishing

the shrine, in time to be framed between two panes
of glass. He cradles a bird in one palm, frozen

and forever watching her, the blush of his face
high on his cheeks. You settle the little house

toward traffic, and we go inside only to stare
from a window. We ask for mercy before we sin.

Motels We Stay in While Trying to Get Pregnant
The Gables

A fresh coat of paint covers everything
and hides nothing, stubby Roman columns
zigzag like teeth along the banisters
and they cut, too, inside my hip bones.
And inside the rooms the walls are empty.
There is nothing beautiful anymore
about my body. We will try again
tomorrow and tomorrow. And we'll fail.
All three nights a child's wail swelters through
the courtyard, and on the third night I leave
our room propped open and put my ear to
door after door frantic to find the cry.
   But I don't. I crawl back to bed, my whole
   torso a clenched jaw waiting to let go.

Motels We Stay in While Trying to Get Pregnant
The Grant

At Christmastime we stay only one night,
and it's a dump — burn holes in brown carpet,
no air. We keep the window open to
the swamp, listen to raccoons and musk rats
pitch in the marsh as they give last fight to
the gators' devouring. The next three
days we drive in separate cars three hours
each way to get to the specialist, up
at 4:00, highway empty and ocean black
on both sides. We drive back after they've coiled
their catheter inside me — the Advent
promise God will not keep. On the last day,
    we surround the nativity, your aunt
      puts Jesus in the manger, and we sing.

Motels We Stay in While Trying to Get Pregnant
The Starlight

An arrow lights up, pointing away from
the hotel, but the metal umbrellas
dotted the roadside, and we knew to turn.
The palms winding to the desk were the same
from the '60s, as we would see carried
over into the bedding, threadbare and
orange. This time, we're eager to see doctors,
but we don't — only nurses — and each night
sitting outside of the bright yellow door
after a day of vials and magic catheters,
we imagine the sunbursts that surround
The Sands echo through my womb, small, ready.
  The phosphenes linger inside for two weeks
  then gone, my gut sinks back into the dark.

Born Under the Veil
for Zaza

The caul means that portion of the amnion which occasionally persists unruptured over the child's head when it is born. Such circumstance was believed by the superstitious of olden times to foretell luck. – International Journal of Medicine and Surgery

My aunt had the caul, Hanrow tells me, his new daughter's
eyes fixed solid on us, *That's how I knew she was in the room.*

She was born face-shrouded in the tissue, emerging from
and into darkness, a sure sign she could see. Not the way

we can. No, our sight is limited. When he was a child
in the city, she brought chickens into the apartment,

where they'd squawk and jerk across the wooden
kitchen floor, competing with his mother's and aunts' voices,

the television, and the oil speaking in tongues, hot in the skillet.
After the dinner, the bones were cleaned and placed in a basket.

Once collected there, she'd throw them, one swift motion,
to where they'd land on the heavy hide mat unrolled

in the living room. Every divination became truth.
He hands his blanketed daughter to me, somehow heavier

than an infant should be, the insight of time far greater
than her few days here, her lineage made clearer by her gift,

announced as this holy hood was peeled from her face
so she could draw her first breath. (This is when he felt

his aunt in the room.) In exchange for the caul, for
entering the world under the curtain of birthright, blind,

she is given second-sight, protection from witches and drowning,
the ability to bring fertile harvests, to transcend.

Born under the weight of these gifts, so much gravity placed
upon her infant form. She makes no sound as she's passed to me.

I bear her weight like water. She never blinks. And I'm both
healed and afraid, so much I fortune cradled to my feeble torso.

the first
rot of autumn from the creek bed below

Tulle

She didn't plan to wear a veil, but decided
she would to take the opportunity to hide

her face in front of the crowd.
So she spent weeks working its mesh

between her fingers, slowly dying it
in teas to reach the perfect shade, dipping

and drying and hanging the dripping piece
on a line in her yard. She found

a rose gold clip in the pocket of a handbag
in her mother's attic and sewed with small

stitches the fabric of her year, affixing it
carefully, just so. When she faced him,

he had trouble lifting it and it tangled
in the wind and caught in her mouth,

but he managed it away from her face
to say what he needed to into her eyes.

Dahlia

The tulle spills over her glittered feet,
her toes gather the dust of the field

where she walks with the man who's already
familiar with her bed in the darkest part

of nighttime. She reaches for a hand
but without smiling, and both breathe

deeper inhaling the perfume of the dahlias
as a petal falls to the rough, hollow grass.

Trim

Because of her age, she shunned white.
She chose silver beads and nude trim,

pinker than the brown of her late-
summer skin. She chose ribbons

that were blue and blush and unraveled
that September, in the storm before

the service. All the flower shops closed
down, so her sisters gathered vines

and flowers in their fists and wound
them tight with wire so they wouldn't

get away from the trellis of her fingers
before they dried crisp in her embrace.

Votive

The light lifted from the front lawn
as the dizzied lovelies took places

on the porch to watch her descend
the stairs, the smell was honeysuckle

and moon, taking its firm place
in the sky after years of nighttime

when it did not rise. The clouds
moved so quickly that the party all

was engulfed in darkness
and the shimmer of votive

without notice. It was hard
to know if it was wedding or vigil

when she hung her head
on his shoulder, brushed a moth

from his collar and breathed in the first
rot of autumn from the creek bed below.

Citadel

The spiral spine of a stairwell twists
toward the tower of the fort

and they are inside its narrow curves,
neither going up to the sky or down

to the chambers of the foundation.
They look at one another and away

from one another as the figure from
the brick atrium flashes light and directs

their embrace, their parting, their kiss.
There is no one else in the citadel,

the guests have gone back to their lives
and the pair is safe, here, in his suit

and her gown, dressed as they were
when they swore words they didn't write

and went home drowsy to tuck each
other into bed, into every night.

When I suggested we go to Vegas for our honeymoon,
this is what I had in mind.

He scrolls photographs of giant arrows
and bigger-than-life sized cowboys,
lightbulbs bulging from their ten-gallon hats
and stars and sunbursts poking the ground

with points that once poked the sky.
People envisioned stars once upon a time
and they all saw them so fascinatingly
differently. The grounded STARDUST

and JACKPOT make us reconsider what it is
to really win something, what it is to want
to touch something you can't so badly
that you settle for its dust. This graveyard

of lightbulbs and steel, dark, yes, but ready
and willing to light up. The rough edges
do not scare us, we prefer the rubble
of what once was to glory. When we arrive,

we will sleep on the ground under teepees made
by old signs promising the chance of fortune.
We will hold each other so tightly despite
the desert heat, and we will know that right now

it is all hope, and along the way we will shine
and we will deceive, and we will not become one
when we become dust, but here, at the beginning,
you can hardly see the end for the glare.

Man of War Harbor
Christmas Tree Island

Aerially, they are white flies on the backs of a turtle. Zoom in
after dusk falls on the east side of Christmas Tree Island,

and they return to homes at anchor, lamps flickering on
inside the cabins, and calls across water like gulls to neighbors.

By day and by land, their dinghies hived like bees in the harbor,
littered with suggestion, crushed aluminum, gas cans, a rain boot.

At night, through a porthole a man takes off sandals and warms
a hot plate, opens a can to expose jagged edges and his dinner,

lies in a slender, low bed on top of a bright Mexican blanket.
Anchored close, a woman waits. Any minute she'll hear the hum

that brings a man home to her, and she tries to reach her toe
to the water where she sits. This is as far as she strays.

Nearer to the mangrove's edge is a man who wades for sea glass
daily, layering each proud piece onto an ever-unfinished mural

that mimics the glass of the ocean inside his cabin. He waits up
nights to watch it. Each mast raises its hand to the sky — not a cry

to be found: a reminder they're there. Layers of drowned boats
beneath them, fixed firm by anchor, free in the elasticity of mud.

In the Eye

The moon is a pit in your stomach
and it grows like swift cancer
in your throat. You can't see it.
You'd swear it's the most perfect day
you've ever lived in, the heron's song
as if for love is clear and reverberates
between the glassy-eyed sea and
the acrylic azure sky.

      But by the time the moon
emerges, the rumors are as swift
and as changed as the churned
ocean approaching. And it is the end.
You go for cover, create a bunker
in your bed, your windows sealed
like a coffin, the night permanent
until the gust has finished having
her way with you. You find the food
in your cabinets that is kept in jars.
You find spoons and the one radio
station that will keep talking
through the fuzz. The lights fail.
But the man's voice keeps on, repeats
the worst of it until it's safe for you
to leave your bed, blink and squint
your eyes in the sun. And then he's
the only sound there is, his static
and relief, until you walk a ways
and see a neighbor you may or may
not recognize. You limbo under
snapped and spitting wire, you
scale the uprooted sidewalk, you
dodge the shingles at your feet
and hear someone say (what a relief
to hear someone say!) you're about

to trip over the white picket impaled
in the almond tree. Nothing is
recognizable. The landscape
of your life doesn't exist anymore.
Houses, shops, docks, and graves:
they're misplaced into abstraction
or altogether gone. Occasionally,
the whir of a generator or a holler
from another end of the island.
You can't believe what you see,
        what you don't see.
You think of the moon again,
what it must feel like to step onto it.
And in this way you conjure it,
call it back to the sky
where it's the only light save
the stars that are tangible braille
in the absence of all messages.
But the moon has changed,
you don't feel it inside anymore.

Almost Home

It's a wasteland.
Metal roofs felled and boats run aground
on the side of the road,
refrigerators, washing machines, rusted out tubs
strewn down this ribbon over the sea,
our road home.

The standing trees have found autumn
in the storm,
in a place that knows no fall.
They've thinned
        and gaping holes expose
                more nakedness.

The palm and mangrove's greens
have seeped into the sea,
they're as brown as if they've burned.

And the boatyards, tiki bars, resorts too.
They've had the wind knocked out of them.
Roofs have been lifted off houses
        and dropped back on, faces peeled back
                to show the dollhouse insides of homes,
aluminum sheets have twisted
        into bowties and shot off windows
                to the roadside.

There are no signs, except the city's
that reminds everyone to be inside
for the night by dusk.
Inside?

Whole trailer parks are parking lots,
their white space a gasp along the road.

Without power, even the houses that still
have insides are really outside.

In the feet of standing water
the mosquitoes have started to swarm
and keep sleep away from the nighttime.

And it's nighttime we pray for,
                              because darkness
is all that looks the same.

You won't want to recall what's been bargained away

Island of Bones

Her poincianas return in flame
outside our window, marking another year
on the island. A few months
with fire in the trees gives way
to tangible air stuck in the throat —
not choking, but silencing.

I've returned again and again to her aerials,
salt pond circles, honeycombed
canals, dry dirt boxes, jagged
metal roofs, knowing that again, I will go,
one day, forever.
                  Still, she bends branches
toward me, offering the sweet red of Surinam cherries,
dropping to the gutter unbroken Spanish limes.

I saw a man ankle-deep in the stench of seagrass,
by the glorious emerald, sapphire, agate and jade.
He was trying to fill a bag full of ocean, but the island
knows better than to give her colors away.

She is not supposed to be easy,
she is not supposed to be forever.

When I am old and perhaps far from here —
finished with it or it all finished —
when I go to remember as my mind finally goes,
there will be there the shapes of coral bodies, beaten
into new forms.
But I will not touch them again.

There will be fire, and I hope
that she will sing to me, recollect in mosaic-songs
of sea glass the music of the exasperated women
and their daily ritual of sweeping
and sweeping
those fallen, sticky petals.

Compound Fracture

I tend to look at the now-mangled arm
when I see the old photographs of us.
It was faultless then: each ligament
defined when you tightened the rope

from the skiff to the dock, every freckle
visible over the contour of your bicep,
your wrist so comfortable in its inversion
when your hand took my hand.

Now the scarring forms letters, I see
different words every time—they spell
the moment when the rope caught,
the wrist snapped, your blood gasped

at the air like the clotted and shocked
pinfish you'd just pulled in. (Did your cast
open like a jellyfish in the sky before it stung
the water and netted the bait?) I imagine

your broken body struggling against the flats —
you threw yourself back, but found
you could only flounder, unable to breathe,
blood and bone in a baptism of salt:

the ache is what reminds you what is pure.

I wonder if fish too feel this way in the air,
on the hook, if they make promises to the water
so the water will take them back, promises
to the air if it will return them to the water.

Now, bits of your body are part of this sea:
the crossroad's price. But so many promises
are forgotten in time. The pain you'll recall.
That limb will never look the way it did

when it moved fingers over my hipbone,
when it whipped and lassoed the fly rod,
when it pressed a palm to my oblique,
when it groped the jaw of the tarpon, caught.

Muscle refusing to flex, the plates and the pins —
these parts will remember. But you won't look back.
You don't want to recall what was bargained away
before the sound of bone splintering on deck.

Dismantling

They're taking off the head of the snake,
and we are watching to remember

what we worry won't exist once we can't
see it anymore. First, they remove the tongue,

slippery from its metal mouth. This is
one of the last of these metal giants,

towering so great that it marks its place
in our memories, doesn't change quick like

the landscape around it. They have packed up
the left edge of the cobra's hood and are moving

their crane to the right. You can see now
that it is empty inside, but when we drove by

again and again — because we wanted to be
taken back to another time — *that time* —

it was solid and permanent. Now
we feel empty, too. They are down

to the coils of the body, the place where
the snake is rooted to the ground —

was rooted. We mourn the soldered bones.
Next door, there used to be an open-mouthed

fish, sucking in the whole sky until the palms
grew unruly and branched into its mouth.

A genie marked the next town over, his blue
face waking the streets from nighttime each day,

until he was taken from his magic carpet,
until the magic was gone altogether. The snake

has been stacked onto a flatbed trailer,
the dirt damp with earthworms beneath

where his body sat before being driven
to a junk yard between stretches of Florida

farm town. We stand on the roadside
and draw with our fingers on the sky

what used to be there, far more looming
now that it is made of emptiness and cloud.

There are no birds on the island, and there was a period in which we'd always talked about this is when the birds would come back. They don't come back now. One of the hurricanes blew them all out to sea. So it was pre-birds, post-birds.

—Gore Vidal, *"Key West, Bohemia in the Tropics"*

Pre-Birds

The hawks draw halos above us
their wings stilled as we are, but soaring.

It's been said they're protectors,
they can see from the air
what we can't
tethered
to the ground.

The white heron in our yard yesterday,
the Greeks would've said, was a sign
from a god —
it frightened me at first,
its unexpected movement.

Then I stood still for a while because of it,
glad for its surprise.

My friend tells me flamingos are the only bird
to, perhaps, disappear from here,
but even that — who knows?

They're meant to symbolize grace,
but I've never seen one with my eyes.

I think of what it would be like without
our birds, and covet the echo
of even those mockingbirds
that grouped and dove
in the fierce shape of an arrow

at our dog. We were too scared
to do anything
but let go
and cover our own eyes.

You say songbirds harbor a grudge
and remember.

Post-Birds

When our neighbor
set his cockatiels free,
it was the first sign
of a town's abandonment —

they'd be blown on wind
beyond their wings
with others more wild —
north to brown winters,
north to where they won't belong
but will inspire awe
in yellow and pink feather
outside the windows of homes
where first fires are started
and the chimneys cough
the first cough of season,
the surprising face
of a spoonbill in New Jersey.

We won't see *our* birds
in the skinny fingertips
of our frangipanis,
except the sturdy pigeons
never swirled away.

We won't see the singing ones either.
The ones we'll see we'll know
don't belong, they're gifts
from Caribbean winds.

We won't want to give them back.
Eventually we will stop
expecting our own birds to return,
we'll satisfy ourselves
in Cuban anthems of new finches.

But there will be a windy day
when we will swear the ocean carries a song
we used to know, a song
we don't remember the words to.
A new hymn echoes
and the birds adapt, we sing
with them when we walk
under gumbo limbo branches.

But we don't count them anymore.
We know that may materialize the gale
that will upturn what now we've come to know,
that we'll have to start counting all over.

Rumors of Tunnels Beneath Us

What if there are tunnels beneath us, their walls
telling stories that lead back further in time

the farther you go into the tightening dark
space to before the town sold its sunlight

when instead it was being built beneath,
at the root – the sugar and spit and blind faith

of belief, the torch light and tobacco, rum
and bone, the silt of coral and splinter of wrecked

ship building a foundation like a secret handshake
for the smugglers and thieves of nighttime?

If there are tunnels, they will be the only way out,
the vaults that hold the history. Above these shafts,

before they've been found — or before they are
no longer kept secret — we collage family stories

and burn the clippings that don't fit with the sun
and a magnifying glass to make ash, to make sense

of roots that only grow above ground.
If there are tunnels, where mysteries move

beneath our neighbors' homes and the whole
of the earth is connected, then a place is left

to origins, a space burns with its people and that
is the only light, casting shadows on what can't be

toured, showing nobody where history is really
rooted, next to glass bottles and barrel planks

and truths told on cold, damp walls, dirt-pattern
narratives safe from the distortion of light.

Viva Voce

When my husband's uncle disappeared
in the middle of the Gulf, his folded jeans

and a silver pistol found on an abandoned
skiff became a story told from Tampa down

through all the islands. His family
could be found in their sleep

meandering the hallways, checking
the bedrooms and sometimes finding

their boy's drenched body in a spare bed
where the ocean deluged from the quilt

to the floor, pushing its way up
the swell-stained walls.

Here, there is always a phonograph tune

you will hear from the sidewalk, coming
from inside the houses, both the inhabited

and the empty ones, where boards dangle,
fat with rot, and metal sheets of roof

are fallen to the footings. This is why
we won't leave here, despite the rising tide

and the growing divide between *then*
and *now* — we are too afraid

of abandoning our dead, and so sure
we will watch our children grow

and die here a thousand times, our bodies
unable to speak, forever telling history.

Emily Schulten is the author of two previous poetry collections, *The Way a Wound Becomes a Scar* (Kelsay Books), a 2023 Eric Hoffer Award Finalist, and *Rest in Black Haw* (New Plains Press). Her poetry and nonfiction appear in *Ploughshares, The Kenyon Review, Tin House,* and *Prairie Schooner,* among others. The recipient of a 2024 Academy of American Poets Laureate Fellowship, she is a professor of English and creative writing at The College of the Florida Keys, and the current Poet Laureate of Key West, where she lives with her husband and her son.

ACKNOWLEDGMENTS

My gratitude to the readers and editors who first selected these poems to appear in these journals and anthologies:

Adirondack Review: "Ode to Fetal Sharks in Jars"
Barrow Street: "Compound Fracture"
The Chattahoochee Review: "Tulle," "Dahlia," "Trim," "Votive," "Citadel" (as "Bride Poem")
Chicago Quarterly Review: "Handling the Wind"
Cimarron Review: "Big Pine Key State Prison"
Colorado Review: "Lovebirds," "Love Poem, Interment"
The Cortland Review: "Motels We Stay in While Trying to Get Pregnant: *The Starlight*"
Crab Orchard Review: "Murmuration"
Dear Human at the Edge of Time: Poems on Climate Change in the US: "In the Eye"
Grist: "Multilingual"
Massachusetts Review: "Ice Diving"
Mayday Magazine: "Sunday Morning"
The Missouri Review: "Born Under the Veil"
Notre Dame Review: "El Lector," "Island of Bones," "The Poem I Can't Write," "Summer Storms"
The Penn Review: "To Make Paradise Out of Paradise"
Ploughshares: "Motels We Stay in While Trying to Get Pregnant: *The Grant*"
Prairie Schooner: "Viva Voce"
Raleigh Review: "Capilla"
Salamander: "Our Life a Stereoscope"
Smartish Pace: "When My Stepbrother Went Missing," "We'll All Be Drowned"
Willow Springs: "Dismantling," "Motels We Stay in While Trying to Get Pregnant: *The Gables*"

"When My Stepbrother Went Missing" is the 2016 winner of the Erskine J. Poetry Prize; "We'll All Be Drowned" was runner-up for the prize in the same year. "Capilla" is one of three pieces of mine that collectively won the 2023 Geri DiGiorno Prize.

The title of this book is a quotation from the novel *Love in a Time of Cholera* by Gabriel Garcia Marquez.

Thank you to my teachers, whose voices are ever-present in my writing and revision, especially David Bottoms, for whose lasting voice I am so grateful. Thank you to my friends who endlessly and confidently support and guide my work, in particular Chelsea Rathburn, James Davis May, and Dionne Irving. Thank you to The Sewanee Writers' Conference, where many of these poems grew strong under the direction of B.H. Fairchild, to whom I owe gratitude as a teacher and friend. Thank you to Sundress Academy for the Arts and Firefly Farms and to the Squaw Valley Community if Writers for the time and space to work on my poems. And thank you to my dear friend Rory Gruler for designing my website.

My deep gratitude to Dennis Maloney, Marc Vincenz, and White Pine Press for their belief in and work on this book.

I am grateful beyond words to my family: my mother, father, and brothers who are the reason I value family dynamics about which I research and write; and the family that Dakin Weekley has given me, who appear so often in these pages and who have felt like my very own since I first met them. I'm further grateful to my island community, where I find support and encouragement from every angle.

Thank you, most of all, to Dakin and to Otis, for making it all worthwhile. You make it all worthwhile.

THE WHITE PINE PRESS POETRY PRIZE

Vol. 29: *Easy Victims to the Charitable Deceptions of Nostalgia* by Emily Schulten. Selected by Marc Vincenz.

Vol. 28: *A Tree Becomes a Room* by J. P. White.
Selected by Danusha Laméris.

Vol. 27: *Blue If Only I Could Tell You* by Richard Tillinghast.
Selected by Joe Wilkins.

Vol. 26: *The Book of Mirrors* by Yun Wang.
Selected by Jennifer Kwon Dobbs.

Vol. 25: *Aflame* by Gary McDowell.
Selected by Sean Thomas Dougherty.

Vol. 24: *Our Age of Anxiety* by Henry Israeli.
Selected by Kathleen McGookey.

Vol. 23: *Secure Your Own Mask* by Shaindel Beers.
Selected by Alan Michael Parker.

Vol. 22: *Bread From a Stranger's Oven* by Janlori Goldman.
Selected by Laure-Anne Bosselaar.

Vol. 21: *The Brighter House* by Kim Garcia.
Selected by Jericho Brown.

Vol. 20: *Some Girls* by Janet McNally.
Selected by Ellen Bass.

Vol. 19: *Risk* by Tim Skeen.
Selected by Gary Young.

Vol. 18: *What Euclid's Third Axiom Neglects to Mention About Circles* by Carolyn Moore. Selected by Patricia Spears Jones.

Vol. 17: *Notes from the Journey Westward* by Joe Wilkins.
Selected by Samuel Green.

Vol. 16: *Still Life* by Alexander Long.
Selected by Aliki Barnstone.

Vol. 15: *Letters From the Emily Dickinson Room* by Kelli Russell Agodon.
Selected by Carl Dennis.

Vol. 14: *In Advance of All Parting* by Ansie Baird.
Selected by Roo Borson.

Vol. 13: *Ghost Alphabet* by Al Maginnes.
Selected by Peter Johnson.

Vol. 12: *Paper Pavilion* by Jennifer Kwon Dobbs.
Selected by Genie Zeiger.

Vol. 11: *The Trouble with a Short Horse in Montana* by Roy Bentley.
Selected by John Brandi.

Vol. 10: *The Precarious Rhetoric of Angels* by George Looney.
Selected by Nin Andrews.

Vol. 9: *The Burning Point* by Frances Richey.
Selected by Stephen Corey.

Vol. 8: *Watching Cartoons Before Attending A Funeral* by John Surowiecki.
Selected by C.D. Wright.

Vol. 7: *My Father Sings, To My Embarrassment* by Sandra Castillo.
Selected by Cornelius Eady.

Vol. 6: *If Not For These Wrinkles of Darkness* by Stephen Frech.
Selected by Pattiann Rogers.

Vol. 5: *Trouble in History* by David Keller.
Selected by Pablo Medina.

Vol. 4: *Winged Insects* by Joel Long.
Selected by Jane Hirshfield.

Vol. 3: *A Gathering of Mother Tongues* by Jacqueline Joan Johnson.
Selected by Maurice Kenny.

Vol. 2: *Bodily Course* by Deborah Gorlin.
Selected by Mekeel McBride.

Vol. 1: *Zoo & Cathedral* by Nancy Johnson.
Selected by David St. John.